ANTHEM
FOR THE WOUNDED

M. A. Vizsolyi

SIBLING RIVALRY PRESS
LITTLE ROCK, ARKANSAS
DISTURB / ENRAPTURE

Sibling Rivalry Press, LLC
PO Box 26147
Little Rock, AR 72221

info@siblingrivalrypress.com

www.siblingrivalrypress.com

ISBN: 978-1-943977-39-0

Library of Congress Control No. 2017942502

This title is housed permanently in the Rare Books and Special Collections Vault of the Library of Congress.

First Sibling Rivalry Press Edition, October 2017

ANTHEM
FOR THE WOUNDED

I. Anthem for the Wounded

II. Goodbye Brooklyn

III. Case Studies

Dedicated to the memory of S. C.,
my friend

I. ANTHEM FOR THE WOUNDED

SIGHT

the little boy ashamed takes his glasses off
steps into the classroom blind & says hello
waving his hand a little at whatever he can
barely see there in four months he will be
dead having gotten lost without his sight in the
woods after school where there was a drop-
off into a limestone valley i still think about
that made-up boy from time to time the dark
color of his eyes his small hands his love of
cartoon bad guys & mini pizzas i suppose i
just want to keep him alive for awhile the boy
who never really was because that's what i
do when aloneness sets in & it helps a little
to know that he's there who never really was
like imagining a nail through your jacket
keeping you safely pinned into the sky when
you were never falling at all but at home on
the ground putting together blocks &
watching cartoons & knowing the little boy
is now tied up with your fate like it or not &
i'll tell you there ain't a lyrical moment in the
world bub that can make that one feel any better

TO A FRIEND WHO ASKED WHY I NO LONGER WRITE LOVE SONNETS

& what would you have me say
now

her whole being
every shape at once
& a bouquet

little golden breasts
like trophies on the page

we could look at them
together
friend

admire
her bedroom manners

the funeral of her halting breath

the way a cape-dove coos

is less beautiful

should i say
something more about her
triumph which i give her
after love's been made

we could move away
outside the window
& watch a one-armed man chasing rabbits

he's not mad

his is a stranger wisdom
than we're used to

but even he
just follows
the atlas
love provides

i know the reason why
the musician of light
no longer plays
at dusk

just now
a perfume

&

because you cannot hear me

because you cannot hear at all

you will never hear me say
that

a great & lovely kiss
has ended

TEMPTATION

consider temptation & pinocchio's nose
extending up to the moon consider the moon
the triumph over sentimentality or my mother
who i love or the triumph over sentimentality
something (gray) slate & quivering a shovel
upright against the blue shed
consider the shovel a glimpse into multitudes
of loss & the father consider the father
i know
you don't care much about the father
or what the bush was feeling when it burned or
even the magician sawing himself in half
you want something other than history
& parlor tricks consider the neck-breaker
his precise measures consider his worship
of the vacuum cleaner or his massage or don't
consider though
the derelict parade all the deflated balloons
& the children running out to walk along
toe-tapping like hors d'oeuvres consider
solitude so necessary
the man with the deflated balloons yells back
from five lines ago i know you though
this whole time you've been considering the father
his shovel his quiet work at dawn
& his thick hands & his boat & his boots
& the way he married terror & laughter
well
the father's done for he's all washed up
so consider yourself
now consider yourself in the fog
you look good in the fog

ONLINE FORTUNE TELLER

you are only mildly visible
in this system

you repeat your name
until your existence
produces small deposits of lime & sand

you would like to be healthier
but there are
enormous quantities
of pudding
at the corner store

haphazardly
you & your love life
are lying in the middle of a country road

it is raining there
there are cows
grazing behind a fence
there are indescribably beautiful maple trees
& hills & a boy
who keeps pulling
an old wagon over you
back & forth

that's his thing

it's just what he does

THE LITHUANIAN WELL

for Johannes Bobrowski

how much of what you do boils down to this
a used car off the lot or a couple of suits
outgrown collecting dust on the shoulders
once you were professor proud carrying
around a book that you've grown to hate
& the clouds were chubbier then & more
fluffy you think when poetry was your all
it reminds you of a story involving the severed
heads of two chimpanzees & the power
those heads wielded how in many ways
the heads became more powerful severed
until they weren't anymore & they decayed
& were forgotten like the lithuanian well
where trout were stored & must have died
some time ago the well trembles when it
hears you coming it remembers that your
song is an unpleasant one to hear that your
song is the tune of the single mother humming
as she hangs her boy's socks on the line her
boy who died many years ago it's an awful
song with its sweetness that carries out &
into the country road the road you must have
passed miles ago where you must have
heard her humming you've made it all that
way saying very little which is something
or you've made it all this way by not being
heard which is something different all together
& so we must believe you when you say coming
into the room empty handed but smiling that
you could write the great poem but don't want to

ANTHEM FOR THE WOUNDED

wounded he said you look wounded when
in the cool afternoon light the blackbird's
tough song reached me where i was
which was near water though only a small
pond clear to the bottom if i could map it

the song & study its movements the way i did as a kid

(though the drawings now look unconvincing from point
to point)

look at how he sends his song at the way i mean
& his face i know the language of that face he is
sad the way language inevitably turns out to be

always (& i'm getting to it)

today i thought of a great big ship sail-less
empty-looking arriving at a rocky coast where three
men come to meet it they are forlorn & worried
(& are their own story too large for now) the ship
runs into the coast & will go down but it is not empty

on the deck sits a small boy
on his head is a red hat
in his hat is a feather & a brooch
in the brooch is an image
in the image
if one looked closely
one would make out a couple holding hands
in his other hand is a bible
in hers a bouquet
in the bouquet are lilies tulips & roses
in the bible is a bookmark with a golden tassel
it marks a place somewhere near the end

when alberto first met isabella he admired her shape & form &
the pressure of her hand on his hand he thought she was like
a sweet dream awakened & he loved her breasts & imagined
them always being near him he even loved her shit & watched
her shit & thought they were like minnows or blessed trout &
stale wine with her at dusk & everything is marvelous & drunk
he once said i love you more than my body will allow & must
sit down & she laughed & isabella loved him but feared that
she did not love him as much as he her & this frightened her &
grew inside of her until she no longer loved him at all & stale
wine was simply stale & she closed the bathroom door & his
love hurt her more & more & sometimes she would sing very
loudly as if to quiet his love & though the melody quite lovely
the words were melancholic & sharp & things went on like this
as they often do & then one day she died & on another day he
died

you look wounded he said the blackbird returns
home on his one good wing saying i was just now
in the garden painting a picture it was a lovely day
& in the picture is a young man who was alone
by the pond quite alone i should say & very quiet
as if at any moment he should hear his name called
by whom i haven't any idea

the detective looking puzzled asked about the old woman
in the background about her empty bird cage her tears (& what
should i have said to him) all she loved i think

it's so lonely here in the garden of fine-backed silence
of breezes which haunt the sun-soaked wood paths of
heavy flowers over-burdened (if you see what i mean)
another field of battle made beautiful & lawn chairs here
& there a fat worm functioning in the grass & we'll never
make it to the wall you should give me your gun
you should rest & sleep & i will come back for you

BABBLING ON HE GRABS MY ARM & ASKS ME WHERE SHE IS

she went out to lean her head on a little
mountain range which she did in the
evening exhausted but restless across
the cracked tiles of the dance hall's bathroom
floor where women gather to piss & laugh
& smoke cigarettes & with no other friend
to talk to i'm out again into the street
every time i see her i suffer i tell the
bouncer sounds bad he says yeah i say
to rescue a plant from being rained on
she went out towards the blue jay holding
it there with its little feet telling me about
the time he said he loved her & how she
never saw him again to hear mint i kneel
down to it it likes the rain & even more
so the way it falls not hard here under
this tree yes she went out dancing i tell
him who is hers that must be where she is

THE MELANCHOLY GARAGE

there's a space in every town
with big weeds
& the loveliness of starved movement

it's like a melancholy garage
with too many antique beer cans
& unfinished projects

sometimes you'll see the place passing
through somewhere in your car
but you'll never stop for it

not out of laziness
you know that once you do there'll be nothing
no magic just weeds

like finding the old man in the garage
he won't even be in the garage
you'll have to look for him in the house

where he sits
watching television
waiting for the mail

FOUR QUATRAINS

What on earth am I to think of a writer who delights
in depicting a living turtle encrusted with precious
stones? I cannot believe that such a person is
worthy of the name of the poet...
                                        – Francis Jammes

how does one write for God chirp because
you will know him chirp on the hillside you will know
the feeling ah yes like a soul smile the homeless
guy said outside of the Odessa chirp then it sleeps

a lattice meaning a set of worn-out dogs black &
white & silvery grey behind the lattice where we sit
together in the city is a kind of shuttling away
of tenderness & down the path with yellow dust

to praise endlessly calm is to truly suffer who
loves you the grandmother kept asking the cat when
it was just the two of us chirp at the piano unlatching
the top & then the light of her presence in blue

i'm thinking about that as if in a vase rather as
though in a vase jealously nurturing her slick & beautiful
stems it brings to mind her charming breasts the little
room enter the little room sigh dejectedly chirp chirp

THE AUCTION HOUSE WHERE WE ARE ON DISPLAY

the casket consumed by lust reached
out trembling recalling old passions
for the two of us on the bench & your
hat which is the color of september just
which was ruling over your sweet face
tipped off or it was the wind unlatching
the screen door off the docks though i
looked back suddenly i'm lost to the
cheap bidding on real distances the man
with the gavel is speaking very quickly
like a young boy trying to describe a game
understanding very well which is song
& a movement of the feet & boundary thus
love thus content the game played out
under the lights of the decrepit field kept on
by some kindness that's free & therefore
incomprehensible entirely i listen
it's all i could do since i could remember
to the dresses of the girls running shiningly
between the boys & gone content
content i keep looking for it looking
back when it was the wind perhaps
& only that at your sweet face hatless
& cold on this beautiful bleak afternoon

I LIKE IT HERE IN AMERICA

i like it here in america we have bellies
consisting of a soft wind over water &
a money tree grown so tall we can no
longer eat its fruit though we can admire
it the way the light catches it at dawn
while you & i friend sit with our coffees
i like it here in america here the birds

innocently sing doo-wop music which
makes us happy almost purely so our
rocks sneeze occasional toxins though
it's not so bad i like it here in america
i'm still allowed to smoke in my back
yard which is nice & when i'm smoking
i'm allowed to enjoy the air if i want to

& we have prettier things here than
anywhere else ourselves look at how we
look at our screens & get so much done
& our hate our hate is more lovely than
moonlight over the seinne now look to
how we say good-bye bow out i like it
here in america perhaps because i do

not read the news for obvious reasons
though mostly because it does not affect
me because i live in fantasy land i like it
here in america we have the moon
which speaks only to us showing off
its bones its perfect speech it spoke to
me last night it had the breath of a mother

CLIP CLOP

from the balcony of footpaths
speak of the black horse
& the dead rider
how old the mirror is which brings with it spirits
like tracks filled with basil
from where you stand
sing an antique song
let your arms veinless hang by your side
wait for the man who took your life away
you will hear his horse
approaching over the bridge
he will come to you as a photograph of himself
you who i dare not name now
who blind has made a bouquet of collapsing temples
& sunflowers
i have no image for what you are to do now
i have brought him to you
i have done all i can

II. GOODBYE BROOKLYN

MCCARREN PARK

little things
carry me
again past
horizons
& foreign
evenings

sometimes i
want to stop
seven times
today &
yesterday two

stop for light
dear lord for
many girls
have mercy
i want to
stop too late
goodbye jane

& mary
goodbye screw
that said jane
& elsewhere
mary too

sad to care
screw that don't
move he said
pointing the
water gun
at my chest
don't you move
dear dear boy

don't move we
are all in
& wild eyes

wheel me off
& you jane
take me home

AFLOAT

on the stairs
time slows down
& the waves
the angled
waves are small
& close i
like the look
of her on
them going
or coming
we take deep
breaths to sit
down with her
on the stairs
now i would
hurry home
what i would
do i would
sail blindly
crash into
them which are
sudden bones
& she would
wait for me
little bird

PROSPECT PARK

farewell sweet
brooklyn where
& who with
sweethearts with
me in the
rain on the
rooftop &
more you stood
to sing when
you were young
something i
remember
your black eyes
in may i
walked over
all of you
in may it
rains a lot
neighborhood
corners with
beer & chips
corners with
wine with booze
& ramen
your house is
still your house
& just as
nice but when
you were young
you seemed to
me older
than now though
less as wise
today it feels
like a long
time ago

MISSUS MITTENS

she only
at last here
too burned my
mouth on them
the greek who
stole my girl
is very
handsome so
right it should
have been you
once i said
on my knees
i could kiss
the hair on
his knuckles

back east though
something's got
to give my
love brings me
everywhere
all i had

the ladies
in the room

i will sing
to you now
i will sing
of flowers
& cooler
evenings
than this one
or beauty
forbidden
to the crook

though missus
mittens loves
him very
much she does

AT THE GATHERING YOU WISH TO LEAVE

you have to
when there are
too many
voices wait
take him he
will i think
his lips do
or move slow
drink your drink
& stop &
don't say to
yourself i
wish to be
away from
this place take
up smoking
& wait moon
now excuse
yourself for
moonlight on
the patio
it's quiet
a fern waits
blindly you
can breathe
escape is
the answer
you notice
few stars there
are maybe
four or five
wait please wait
for me love
i am on
my way to
be away

with you &
laugh in the
nothingness
of a large
& incredibly
empty room

BENEATH THE FENCE

i find i
am no more
mad i am
this face this
lovely face
remember
thinking it
which never
was sweet love
i'm close to
song but not
this life the
will of light
now & her
form in the
water bend
down to see
feet on the
other side
of the fence
her secret
vein there all
was applause
she was mine

DERBY DAY

there's something
sweeter than
sunlight i
said leaving
it for this
dark bar with
drinks to watch
the horses
run ronnie
i said *you*
watch no one
is going
to beat this
two horse he
just looks so
peppy &
they say he's
a sure bet
three minutes
later the
two horse won
so you won
he asked me
no I had
the five why
because he
is a born
loser i
could picture
him losing
so clearly
the slow start
the bump on
the rail the
exhausted
& lonely

finish you
find a horse
like that &
you make your
donation

FOR JULIE KENT

julie kent
in almost
anything
is something
that i love
it's in her
face as she
looks down at
turned out feet
something far
away &
a house in
the country
with kids she
no longer
loves maybe
her husband
is sending
letters from
the ukraine
he went there
& never
came back she
anywhere
would be just
as lovely
even there
i thought that
night watching
her twice-lithe
body fall at
last & down

GOODBYE BROOKLYN

i listened
to john for
a while on
the stoop of
his building
saying the
city's gone man
i lived here
my whole life
& can you
believe it
i get lost
now sometimes
no more ben's
deli no more
pop's pizza
& no more
average
joes like joe
he's gone too
i return
home from work
to find that
my home went
missing i
put up signs
but only
young people
call asking
how much is
it & is
there a nice
cafe nearby
i tell them
there are a
number of

wonderful
places to
sit down &
have coffee
& then i've
sold my home
& taken
my family
somewhere far
away & there
are no nice
cafes there just
a park with
no trees you
know what i
mean i nod
my head &
say yeah man

HAUNTED HAYRIDE

lips being
everything
i was with
desire &
you were there
high up on
the roof of
june playing
musical
buildings with
the pigeons
& frank fired
from the store
was there &
all was as
if upon
hay good &
warm & word
by word we
won out in
overtime a
day game at
shea in the
wagon on
its way out
of brooklyn
we were scared
enough to
scream out loud
screaming bee!
bee! ah! bee!

FOR MARY WHO TENDS BAR

mary to
defend her
only self
weaponized
beauty the
oak tree &
herself she
used a dress
& beauty
all she has
to defend
now
      how is
mary if
you see her
there at the
cafe loup
if you see
her do not
tell her i'm
coming so
lovely she
when alone
when surprised
oh yes &
most of all
then to see
me & you
&
    yes all
she has now

WITH THE ART STUDENT

if the boys
are teeth i
said looking
at his dark
painting of
school boys at
recess in
the yard of
the school then
what do they
eat you tell
me he said
box organs
i said or
the souls &
ambition
of young school
teachers all
across the
country you
tell me i
can't he said
& looked down
& looked sad
in any
event there
they are yes
he said there
they are

ON THE EAST RIVER FERRY

only the way
lovelier
this & calm
& mine i
was ill but
real watch out
for my bags
they're leaving
my hands were
on a dream
demons dream
deeply them
i combed
did buy one
bought more &
more & more
thursday was
here & i
loved it then
i had no
speech or guilt
barcelon-
a you seem
also mazed
strange hallway
where a friend
must be no
reason just
the beauty
of the sea

HELLO HOW ARE YOU HAVE A NICE DAY

*hello how are
you have a
nice day* was
all he said
ever &
just like that
he never
did get much
better for
a while he
was outside
again with
his hand on
his railing
looking down
& smoking
cigarettes
he never
did look up
not for me
saying hi
or the girls
across the
street serving
beers he was
looking bad
that last time
i saw him
buy a pack
he stopped in
the middle
of the street
& lit one
up & stared
at it for
a while he

never did
get better
god he loved
cigarettes
when he died
he took them
with him smoked
them right up
to the gate
stopped & with
his head down
said to saint
pete *hi how*
are you have
a nice day

UNDER THE BQE

under the
BQE
are a lot
of dead birds
i try to
avoid them
walking home
but it's hard
their pulpy
violet
innards catch
the side of
my eye &
the day is
ruined i
wonder whose
job it is
to clean up
under the
overpass
maybe it's
no one's i'd
do it of
course but there's
just so much
of it &
so many
dead birds there
i couldn't bear
to hold them

DUMBO

let's all walk
forever
under it
the sweet sky
almost bed
time though for
a few more
hours with you
if i had
to i would

there are no
pretty girls
here can a
poet find
a muse in
this damn hell-
hole reading
lately ted
an old tune
& shaking
good for now

& it might
be too late
for us well
oh well &
damn it all

ON THE TOMBSTONE OF A HORSE

i am a
horse who wrote
this poem
i don't care
what you think
or believe
a horse is
what i am
to know the
rider well
is an art
too & can
be written
down she is
beautiful
who took a
stick to my
side & pulled
my hair &
i took her
places at
such speeds &
heard her laugh
joy was all
then did bring
us down once
falling in
a hole &
being put
down i called
out to her
saying i
praise you
& am not
mad this is
life to be

given to
you & to
be undone
by you too

PERHAPS WHEN BROOKLYN'S GONE

perhaps when
Brooklyn's gone
whoever
whatever
is left here
will at a
loss for words
sit where i
am sitting
i'm also
at a loss
for words i'm
responding
to the news
which says that
soon any
day now it
could happen
it's not that
that bothers
me so much
what's always
anyway
& it must
be more to
this tree here
in the park
seeing a
young man pass
by his hands
behind his
back his head
down thinking

VAN BRUNT

lost song &
afternoon
storms over
head the rain
asleep for
now when asked
to question
the hurried
furious
love kisses
the young do
i refuse
so what how
sweet they are
& you were
sweet & i
am alone
& thinking
about them
the young &
you & a
song that i
lost & rain
which has come

GREENPOINT

i like to
be passing
by the church
& see the
polish at
mass it's so
crowded in
there they stand
outside the
doors are wide
open & the
kids can't help
but look out
at the park
& think of
ice cream &
the fountain
often i'm
on my way
to buy kale
two bags of
it often
i forget
why i want
it go to
the taco
place & then
order two beers
two shots of
tequila
three tacos
& feel love
in my heart

OPERATION ACCEPTABLE LOSS

the way you
keep flowers
makes it noon
& the kids
are outside
playing war
the germans
are winning
again they
are always
winning at
noon bonbon
lillies &
violets
as if they
weren't a
luxury when
a time of
war the kids
are saying
is no time
to dispute
whether or
not you are
dead if i
say i shot
you dead then
dead you are
so die with
honor &
no cheating

BRIGHTON BEACH

we sing the
shore & mist
& with our
faces i
approach her
i say you
are my tone
console me
when madame
bovary
near the lit
fire with tea
extends her
left arm &
hand with rings
i feel most
alone &
even on
the beach &
even with my
love the low
light of lamps
they are dim
worlds i am
with helmet
on in them
my lungs do
not move the
shore is far
away now
what do *you*
do when the
shore is far
away now

III. CASE STUDIES

THE CASE OF POPPIES AND H.D.

Was that her just now
squeezing into my ear
& running through a field of poppies
in a poem no one
not even in a million years
will have the nerve to say
that poppies are single kisses turned to stone

but what are kisses to us
speak the poppies
the bearers of forgotten desire
if anything
we are small secret altars to ourselves

& i find her
she is halfway beautiful
in her tiered evening dress
of green & yellow fabric
she is sleeping in the field of poppies
& whispering to herself:

in the movie i would be heartbroken forever

laying in a bed very far from a field of poppies

where someone has laid a trap

dropping a single poppy in a snare

which is inconspicuous & perfect

laughter from somewhere in the elms

which border this field of lovely poppies

i believe them to be young demons

beautiful & pure & troubled.

THE JUNKMAN STRUGGLES

& this no one will buy it foil-plated &
worn a few handkerchiefs made for
those whose words sound like a soft
electric snare now & even here in
the city where junk is in i struggle
& sometimes harry comes by with
a sandwich from frank's & a beer &
he found a big chunk of ugly wood
leaning up against a fence asked
if i could maybe sell it as a table or
something nah wood's out i tell him
it has to be so impractical as to be
truly ironic something iron an axle
off a car we could mount it to this
ugly ass piece of wood & sell it as
artwork they like that kind of stuff
it doesn't make sense to me or you
but it gives them pleasure but i'm
just too damn lazy i'm a true junkman
which means my shit's junk when
harry leaves i like to play some music
something by ellington maybe or
parker i like to lay down on the
concrete floor & make little noises
with the music while the customers
laugh at len fuller & his radio

ARCHIE WHO LIVES IN MADNESS LAND

i knock weeping at the house of the genius
& leave you messages via cell phone his yard
has many junipers & an old pick-up truck &
a metal fence that curls at the bottom & a hot-air
balloon a great big one & fog that tries for melody
but fails & salamanders in a creek & a horse
belongs here too lame glistening in a field
behind me like a special absence & i just want
to say that i'm sorry about all the messages
but his ecstasies this field & the boy in the yellow
cab with his head down

SIX EXPLANATIONS

for Ronnie Yates

there was an old man over there i think he's dead now
a young couple moved into his house they have a little girl
who plays in the backyard where he used to sit & yell *shut-
up* at the birds

& as to why he yelled?

i'm thinking he was a failed composer & the pure & perfect
song of the birds mocked his life's work his own clumsy
attempts at music

i'm thinking his wife who used to every morning put fresh
water in the birdbath who used to keep the feeders filled
has died & the birds who do not understand this ask for her
may they say *may*

i'm thinking or the birds are tiny demons who try to torture
with their song & their smallness us though only he could see it

i'm thinking there's one particular bird the teller of some long
& secret epic parsed out each day that he was listening to that
the others were distracting him from

or he loved their song their symphony so much so that he
wanted to add to it but full of & understanding only anger
shut up was the only melody he had

i'm thinking more likely there was something else he was trying
to hear but what sound or voice so quiet or so far away as to be
trumped by them who singing is very quiet if shrill in backyards
in those towns that have them

THE CASE OF BRIDGET

i'm going to
let you in on something
i overdo everything
i can't help it
even this poem is getting away from me
at any moment there might be
three or four tiny birds singing in the bathtub
the cat on pointe
maybe a squirrel
or a duck doing something contrary to its nature
& you're sure to find
a heavy child
weeping beside a pink dress
her eyes will be puffy & swollen
you'll know her right away
from the way she braids her hair
& pins it back up
you should go up to her if you have the time
& give her a tissue
she's really such a sweet girl
she will look up at you
from beneath her crossed arms & disappear
i don't know where she went or why
it's unimportant
what's important is that you're here now
you made it
we can do whatever you'd like
we can even do nothing
it's so nice to do nothing
to just sit & wait
for the light to drain out of the room

ANOTHER POEM FOR JOY

is it the same joy as the one who
half mad or completely tried to
fuss with the wires of the school
bus saying i hope you all die if
not today then soon she was like
a living room assembled in a green
garden with couches & lamps &
all & for no real reason just because
the owner said when i sat down on
the garden couch & sipped my tea
where are we i asked her not where
love is & then right where love is
like a child on a swing who upwards
smiles downwards frowns & his
mother with her bad sleep & her
no sex looks past him the car door
slams & the father a cigar in his
mouth smiles & it was joy i was trying
to tell you about her blonde hair she
liked to watch the movie *grease* & if
you try & turn it off she said i'll kill
you & i'll make it hurt real bad

THE CASE OF STANLEY K. ON RIVER ROAD

there is one memory
i have from that period
you
& the way the light was
you didn't believe
she was of this world
the world
being what it was
when it reached you
on the porch
Mr. Thompson's granddaughter
jumping rope
love is more discriminant
when you're young

somewhere it was raining
people were laying on their sofas watching *e.t.*
somewhere an automobile
was being hauled away for good

JUST ANOTHER SAD, SAD EVENING

you've come back again
looking for the weeping girl
with braids
you most likely
have a better phrase
or feel more prepared to deal with sorrow
she's still gone
i put her in a bar
she is older & thinner
& more beautiful
& is a stripper
i can take you to see her
if you'd like
but i don't think
she'll want to speak with you
she's grown colder
& cries less
but we can watch her dance
i can even arrange for something
more private
if that's the kind of thing you'd be interested in

THE GOLEM BRED FOR WAR

1. *his pitiful dreams*

on the foot of the bed in the late afternoon the magician
        fingering his deep red cape

outside the woman with the musical saw a dirge or an
        anthem for her other half

the slick but very simple minded philosophies of the
        poets marching past

the squirrel an acorn in his hands watching from his
        throne of nuts

an army of lavender surrounding her smile asleep in the
        field of men

the majesty & beauty & terror of two hundred horses
        emerging from the ocean

so the thread dissolving in blue liquid the audience their
        antique clothing applauding generously

a veil over the new building reading litschansky
        construction company & believe

whether or not it was morning the violence of the fine
        weather rocking the tall grass

the pump pumping its oozy something into the street

the trenches in the distance like the sticky shadows of
        large birds

the cannon firing off loose change & peaches which grow
        below the hill near water

celia leaning on the iron gate smoking a sign of rain said
    captain elegy

the picture on the milk carton a sandal in black & white

the magician looking out the window all alone now just
    the rabbit his constant twitching

awaiting you are three graves the mystic said the french
    poodle in her lap

the instinct to cower suddenly & tuck & roll

the mortician's dark joke the suggestion box in the
    morgue

what's needed to face the empty face which greets you
    on these bitter days

2. *the golem for war buys flowers*

the golem loved her very much she is soooo
wunderbar he said buying violets from the blind
woman & can you describe her for me the woman
said fingering some loose change yes he said
                                                       she
like me belongs to the magician & i love both halves
of her her top half which when I speak to it laughs
& shakes the arms opening like two armies making
way for the assault of her kisses on my face & her
breasts which are two stars arguing about the grief-
ridden songs of amorous birds
                                       & the golem needing
to use his hands put down the flowers adjusted his
glasses her lower half he said is here & quickly gone
& sometimes i place my head into the pillow it creates
& kiss the pillow & lift it up & cause it to sing like
this: & the golem sang the song of her lower half which
was like water suddenly set free & crashing into
the tower where the ancient violins are stored
                                         & the woman
smiled a little remembering something or other from
another lifetime
                             & the golem said but what i love more
than each half is each half together & in my arms &
carrying her from the world of the wooden box into
the next one where secret filaments chart out the
movement of wind which carries the dust off our bodies
                                         the blind
woman seeing their love cried
                                 then she sang a little
gypsy tune about water & immortality & died

3. *the golem moves on*

when love comes with her ghostly ribbons

the flickering of swinging lamps & the moths

or the submissive & ashen face of the salesman in drag

with a blanket & red wine in paris hilda alone near the river

two galloping colts one called lucky rainbow

outside a parking lot shrine to autumn the leaf blower

the cat killing the bulldog under the big lights

but still forgiveness the rooftop fallen in the mouse's paradise

& still forgiveness in that voice of hers

piano keys in the garage of cadmus the phoenician

everything's soft only just everything

not understanding the people's small voices struggling to make
    sound

like this sound merely a ghost of disapproval

in the kennel we'd be happy says hilda by the roadside to the
    man who never dies

he goes on where gleams the branches in midwinter

he goes on singing a lullaby for the stockbroker's wife

he brings her flowers & makes love to her & buries the little
    mouse out back

LOW SOUNDS

a whole day went by through the window
in half-light & i watched the old woman
making tea she was bald & did not put her
teeth in (for whom no need) not for this
poem which asks us to keep it down the

music it's what we can take away on our
rowboats through driftwood then almost
silence there & i stop rowing the wind shifts

its fluttering & stops again the tiny waves
subside slowing down like tired dancers at
a ball & i look into the window again i like to sit

in the dark & think about the madness of water

THE CASE OF THE COUPLE

yesterday i sailed on out of the city in
a small boat with a small but sweet crew
of two they wanted me to take them to
Jersey which wasn't far & would make
for a nice trip the thin clouds kept the sun
at bay & the wind was just right & the
sound of the sail was soft as we moved
away when we reached the other side i
told them to go on ahead of me i was
right behind them & then i left them
in Jersey i backed the boat out it was
quiet i wanted just then & nothing
was going to stop me from sailing out
to sea for just a bit & going for a swim

FINAL THOUGHT (OR WHAT I MEANT TO TELL YOU)

time happens turning loose somewhat small unknown joys
but that's not what i meant to tell you about just things
getting too far away from me i remember the deep cry
of seawater when errors sent me to the shore at night the bay
rotating i thought in a cup on a pin small & private & it was
errors i mean to say the kind that poetry is not for

it's true that there are things poetry can not hold
it's a secret tension that turns cold &

then forgets you or a light too much like light i meant to say

ACKNOWLEDGMENTS

I would like to thank the editors of the following journals where many of these poems first appeared, often in earlier versions:

Bomb, Diagram, Epiphany, Fourteen Hills, Gulf Coast, Harpur Palate, The New Orleans Review, Ninth Letter, Pleiades, Ploughshares, Spinning Jenny, THEthe Poetry, Transom.

ABOUT THE POET

M. A. Vizsolyi is previously the author of *The Lamp with Wings: love sonnets*, (HarperPerennial) winner of the National Poetry Series, selected by Ilya Kaminsky. He is also the author of the chapbooks, *Notes on Melancholia* (Monk Books) and *The Case of Jane: A Verse Play* (500places press), which was produced for Performa 13 and broadcast on NPR. Vizsolyi's work can be found in numerous journals, including *The New Orleans Review, Narrative, Crazyhorse, Cream City Review, The Journal, Pleiades, The Burnside Review, Harpur Palate, Ninth Letter, Ploughshares*, and *Gulf Coast*. He is part of the faculty of the BFA in Creative Writing Program at Goddard College and faculty advisor for the college's national literary journal, *Duende*. He lives in Santa Barbara, California.

ABOUT THE ARTIST

Annalisa Barron is an artist and filmmaker currently working in Brooklyn, NY. She graduated from Penn State University with a BFA in Painting and Drawing in 2013 and with an MFA in Sculpture from the Pratt Institute in 2017. Her short films include *The Kingdom of Back* (2017), *E.V.E.: Erectus Vegetabilis Evitaneous* (2013), *Incarnate* (2013) and *Chair Man* (2012). Her work has been exhibited at the Cooper Union, El Minia University, the U.S. Embassy in Nicaragua and the NO/GLOSS film festival in Leeds, UK. (www.annalisabarron.com)

ABOUT THE PRESS

Sibling Rivalry Press is an independent press based in Little Rock, Arkansas. It is a sponsored project of Fractured Atlas, a nonprofit arts service organization. Contributions to support the operations of Sibling Rivalry Press are tax-deductible to the extent permitted by law, and your donations will directly assist in the publication of work that disturbs and enraptures. To contribute to the publication of more books like this one, please visit our website and click *donate*.

Sibling Rivalry Press gratefully acknowledges the following donors, without whom this book would not be possible:

TJ Acena	Randy Kitchens	Paul Romero
Kaveh Akbar	Jørgen Lien	Robert Siek
John-Michael Albert	Stein Ove Lien	Scott Siler
Kazim Ali	Sandy Longhorn	Alana Smoot Samuelson
Seth Eli Barlow	Ed Madden	Loria Taylor
Virginia Bell	Jessica Manack	Hugh Tipping
Ellie Black	Sam & Mark Manivong	Alex J. Tunney
Laure-Anne Bosselaar	Thomas March	Ray Warman & Dan Kiser
Dustin Brookshire	Telly McGaha & Justin Brown	Ben Westlie
Alessandro Brusa	Donnelle McGee	Valerie Wetlaufer
Jessie Carty	David Meischen	Nicholas Wong
Philip F. Clark	Ron Mohring	Anonymous (18)
Morell E. Mullins	Laura Mullen	
Jonathan Forrest	Eric Nguyen	
Hal Gonzlaes	David A. Nilsen	
Diane Greene	Joseph Osmundson	
Brock Guthrie	Tina Parker	
Chris Herrmann	Brody Parrish Craig	
JP Howard	Patrick Pink	
Shane Khosropour	Dennis Rhodes	

www.ingramcontent.com/pod-product-compliance
Lightning Source LLC
LaVergne TN
LVHW010308070426
835512LV00024B/3481